My Jesus

Reflections *of the* Redeemer

JANICE K. POWELL

Copyright © 2025 by Janice K. Powell

All rights reserved.

A publication of Words Beyond Me Press.

No part of this publication may be reproduced, distributed, or transmitted in any form or by any means, including photocopying, recording, or other electronic or mechanical methods, without the prior written permission of the publisher, except as permitted by U.S. copyright law.

Cover & interior design by Typewriter Creative Co.
Cover & interior artwork by Kaylyn Powell Stacy

ISBN 979-8-9936772-1-7 (Hardcover)

ISBN 979-8-9936772-6-2 (eBook)

Introduction

A Title

On these pages you will discover 366 life-changing, one-sentence declarations that begin with these two powerful words: *My Jesus*. *My*—because He is so personally dear to me and is everything my soul needs, and *Jesus*—because His is the Name that is above all names. Forever exalted. Forever mine.

A Story

Early in 2017, I shared on social media a *My Jesus* declaration to testify to the Lord's power and to declare in faith what I believed He could and would do for me. To my delight each day after that, another declaration proclaiming the character of my Savior welled up within me. Days became weeks, weeks became months, and months became nearly two years of daily posts.

The collection has since grown to almost 900, each one a personal testimony of gratefulness, biblical truth, and awe. Though these words did not begin life as a book, I am thrilled they have become one. I look forward to rejoicing with you as these truths and this glorious hope help create your My Jesus story in the coming year.

An Invitation

Each day you will encounter facets of the Lord's character through a statement paired with scripture references, or you will engage in a prayer that complements the day's reading. This uncomplicated format invites you to study, reflect, and journal as the Holy Spirit leads. Each reflection serves as a springboard for embarking on your own journey of formulating or confirming your beliefs. For further study ideas, consider Suggestions for Going Deeper, p. 451.

A Presence

Some statements you may already know to be true, while others may not yet be part of your experience. If the latter, you may express them as prayers. Each of us is at a different place on the Lord's path as He leads us home. Through the challenges on my path, He demonstrates His character and assures His presence. He faithfully carries me, gently encourages me, and powerfully anchors me in truth. He is faithful to do the same for you on your path.

A Prayer

May this year's journey bless you with peace, assurance, greater faith, wonder, and even questions that compel you to delve more deeply into the character and attributes of Jesus. May you bask in His presence as you ponder the reflections, pray the prayers, search scripture, and discover other attributes for yourself. May you lean into Him as He draws you ever closer to His heart, and may you rejoice that He holds yours.

A Purpose

If you are that one person who weeps tears of joy over a truth that transforms your faith and changes your life, know that I thought of you and wept for you as I wrote. But more importantly, our Jesus did. And He thinks of you now, loves you, draws you—at this moment and always. May the words within these pages and the scriptures you encounter enhance your awareness of His everlasting goodness, tender care, and eternal hope.

All for Him,
Janice

At Your Table

You invite me to Your table
Pull out my chair
Bid me sit in Your presence.

I come thirsty, yearning
You pour living water
And overflow my cup.

Table brims with holy fare
And sparkling water of life
Abundant and freely given.

I come empty, hungry for hope
You inspire, refresh, sustain
My soul revels in the filling.

In Your presence nothing lacks
My spirit thrives, replete
With life and light and love.

Let me ever dine with You
Let me ever linger
At Your table always bid me stay.

Janice Powell

Day 1

My Jesus

can renew a languishing spirit, transform a troubled life, and create a new beginning at any moment, no matter the day or year, because His grace, mercy, and power transcend clocks and calendars.

2 Peter 3:8

Habbakuk 1:12a

2 Thessalonians 2:16-17

Day 2

My Jesus
teaches me that forgiveness restores relationships, joy triumphs over bitterness, and His unconditional love heals and delivers the wounded, angry spirit.

Colossians 3:12-14
John 15:11
Ephesians 4:31-32

Day 3

My Jesus
calls me to trust Him implicitly, surrender to His supremacy, and continually seek His will so that I may walk in peace, humility, and holiness.

Psalm 4:5
James 4:7
Isaiah 55:6

Day 4

My Jesus
is the fulfilling, untainted, and life-giving opposite of everything this depraved world offers.

Lord,

Thank you for completely satisfying the desires of my heart. Thank you for helping me understand how very opposite of the world you are, a truth that helps me focus on and live for what lies beyond. May I never be satisfied with the world but ever satisfied with you.

Amen.

Day 5

My Jesus
knew I could never meet His standard of righteousness on my own, so He gave me His righteousness—a costly gift indeed.

Romans 3:23
Isaiah 61:10
Psalm 49:8

Day 6

My Jesus
draws the empty one to His living water,
the broken one to restoration, and the
wayward one to His everlasting truth.

John 4:10
Psalm 23:3
Psalm 117:2

Day 7

My Jesus
bestowed such love upon mankind
that every moment He suffered, every
mockery He endured, and every mercy
He extended transpired according
to His choice, His obedience to the
Father, and His selfless sovereignty.

Matthew 26:39
Matthew 27:29
Colossians 1:16

Day 8

My Jesus
fills me with peace as He removes worry, leads me into contentment as He removes unrest, and transforms me with hope as He removes despair.

Matthew 6:31-33
Philippians 4:6-7
Hebrews 13:5

Day 9

My Jesus
speaks to me in words that soar from the pages of my Bible to be painted on the canvas of my mind, inscribed on the tablet of my heart, and imprinted on my soul.

Lord,

Thank you for your word that speaks to my mind, heart, and soul as it comforts and refines me in ways that change me forever. No other book can boast of such power and promise. No other words speak life. No other words are life.

Amen.

Day 10

My Jesus
teaches me through His inerrant and unchanging word that there is not this truth or that truth, his truth or her truth, my truth or your truth, but only the truth.

Malachi 3:6
John 14:6
2 Timothy 3:16

Day 11

My Jesus
astonishes me with how starkly but sublimely His eternal hope contrasts with the despair that would have consumed me had He not shown me irresistible kindness and forbearance.

Psalm 34:18
2 Thessalonians 2:16-17
Psalm 27:13

Day 12

My Jesus
encourages me to know more of Him than
I did yesterday, to trust Him more today
than ever before, and to walk in His peace
and power every moment trusting that
His words are dependable and true.

Ephesians 4:14-16
Psalm 115:11
Romans 15:13

Day 13

My Jesus
took all my sin upon His shoulders and forever erased the record against me so not the faintest mark of condemnation remains.

Psalm 103:12
Colossians 2:13-14
Psalm 103:10

Day 14

My Jesus
is my protector who helps me navigate the waters of this life, my compass who keeps me on course, and my strong deliverer who carries me safely to His bright and peaceful shores.

Lord,

I am grateful that you guide me and that someday I will step into the Promised Land where all is bright and peaceful because you are there. Thank you for your faithful, calming presence here, and thank you for your promise to bring me safely home to you.

Amen.

Day 15

My Jesus
invites all who are crippled by sin and deserving of death to dine with Him at the King's table and be healed, filled, and made alive forever.

2 Samuel 9:10
Romans 6:23
Revelation 19:7-9

Day 16

My Jesus
teaches me to recognize fearful situations and worrisome unknowns as opportunities for Him to show me yet again that His power is enough.

Psalm 27:3

Isaiah 12:2

Luke 12:7

Day 17

My Jesus
is the God who heals and beautifies as
He creates wholeness from heartache
and brings blessings from brokenness.

Psalm 147:3
Ecclesiastes 3:11
Job 42:12

Day 18

My Jesus
expects nothing from me for which
He does not also supply His presence
and power to accomplish.

Psalm 121:1-2
2 Peter 1:2-3
Philippians 1:6

Day 19

My Jesus
shows me that there is no room for envy, worry, or bitterness in a heart overflowing with joy in Him.

Lord,

I trust you to continue giving me a more joyful heart as you heal the brokenness sin has caused. Thank you for your powerful provision as together we root out all envy, any worry, and every bitterness. Thank you for loving me enough to sanctify me.

Amen.

Day 20

My Jesus
is as faithful when I doubt as He is when my faith can move mountains—always able, always present, always true.

Psalm 43:5
Psalm 36:5
2 Timothy 2:13

Day 21

My Jesus
knows every detail of every circumstance of my life, and before time began, He divinely orchestrated all for my good and His glory.

1 John 3:20b
Psalm 37:23
John 8:58

Day 22

My Jesus
instructs me to look to Him for vindication and justice rather than to man and the world's broken system.

Psalm 35:27
Deuteronomy 32:35-36
Proverbs 28:5

Day 23

My Jesus
is heaven's antidote to greed and selfishness
as He encourages instead a humble generosity
that magnifies His presence in the believer.

1 Timothy 6:18-19
Matthew 6:2-4
James 3:16

Day 24

My Jesus
is the only remedy for broken spirits,
hearts that have lost all hope, and eyes
that cannot see a way through the pain.

Lord,

Thank you for not leaving us hopeless or helpless. Instead, you abundantly pour out love and healing for those who earnestly seek you. Help me to recognize those who yearn for what you offer and to share with them your hope.

Amen.

Day 25

My Jesus
has done everything for me, yet one day He will welcome me into His presence and give me the crown of life as if I had done anything worthy of such a gift.

James 1:12
Luke 23:43
Romans 6:23

Day 26

My Jesus
is always attuned to my contrite and humble prayers, and He demonstrates with every answer His tenderhearted care and limitless power to act beyond my imagination.

Psalm 65:2
1 Peter 5:7
Ephesians 3:20-21

Day 27

My Jesus
is working when I cannot see Him,
forgiving when I do not deserve it, and
fighting my battles when all seems lost.

Psalm 121:4

Psalm 103:10

Exodus 14:14

Day 28

My Jesus
teaches me that although I am never without sin this side of eternity, I am forever free of condemnation because He forgave me, and His righteousness became mine.

1 John 1:8
Romans 8:33
Romans 8:1

Day 29

My Jesus
exhorts me to be still and know that His love for me, His power over my circumstances, and His infinite knowledge are far greater than any problem I will ever encounter.

Lord,

Your love comforts me. Your power over every circumstance and your limitless knowledge give me strength to face the next moment. I am at peace with whatever lies around the next bend because you—my all-powerful and all-knowing Savior—are already there.

Amen.

Day 30

My Jesus
teaches me that in the power of His Spirit,
I am to speak the truth in love and act
as He would act, no matter the deceitful
words or hateful actions of others.

Ephesian 4:15
1 Corinthians 13:4-8a
1 Thessalonians 1:6

Day 31

My Jesus
mercifully forgave my sin, graciously brought me into vibrant fellowship with Him, and daily empowers me to forsake sin and pursue holiness.

Romans 5:8
Isaiah 55:7
2 Corinthians 7:1

Day 32

My Jesus
is my focal point as I look to the future
and trust that He will bring me safely to
that triumphant moment in His presence
when my faith will be made sight.

Hebrews 12:1-2
1 Timothy 6:19
Hebrews 10:23

Day 33

My Jesus,
who formed molecules, mountains, and galaxies by the word of His mouth, has the power to speak truth, life, and light into my soul.

Psalm 33:6
Luke 11:36
John 1:4

Day 34

My Jesus
equips me to persevere through both the routine and the unforeseen and helps me trust that my days are ordered and numbered by Him alone.

Lord,

Thank you for the assurance that you have ordered all my days—even the messy, not-as-I-planned days—and you give me the strength to persevere through each of them. The power and peace of such assurance is priceless.

Amen.

Day 35

My Jesus
is the everlasting truth that quiets my heart, counsels my mind, and anchors my soul in the midst of worldly clamor and spiritual turmoil.

Psalm 119:160
Psalm 16:7
Hebrews 6:19

Day 36

My Jesus
comforts, strengthens, and settles my soul as I cling to Him and joyfully receive exactly what I need.

Psalm 63:8
Psalm 86:17
Psalm 119:16

Day 37

My Jesus
is the immovable foundation and
indestructible fortress that keeps me
safe and holds me steady through
every quake and storm.

2 Timothy 2:19
Psalm 18:2
Psalm 46:2-3

Day 38

My Jesus
gently searches my heart and examines my thoughts to align my inmost being with His character.

Psalm 139:23-24
Psalm 139:3
Proverbs 16:2

Day 39

My Jesus
urges me to focus on learning who He is, and as I do, I discover and flourish as the person He created me to be.

Lord,

Your word instructs me to become like you, so please help me know who you are. Teach me your character and your ways, help me grow in my relationship with you, and shape me into the person you want me to be.

Amen.

Day 40

My Jesus
proves that self-empowerment is worthless in the face of circumstances beyond human control and that true power is found only in Him.

Romans 12:3
2 Corinthians 12:9-10
Matthew 6:27

Day 41

My Jesus
is my only hope for entering His presence,
and He has mercifully reached down to lift
me up to where I cannot go on my own.

Romans 5:6
1 John 4:19
1 John 5:12

Day 42

My Jesus
speaks over the chaos and clatter of
this world to assure me that He alone
is my peaceful, quiet refuge.

Psalm 46:10

Psalm 57:1

John 16:33

Day 43

My Jesus
bestows wisdom as He removes foolishness, love as He overcomes hate, and freedom as He defeats that which enslaves.

James 1:5
Mark 12:31
Romans 6:17-18

Day 44

My Jesus
always answers my prayers and always works on my behalf whether I recognize His actions immediately or in retrospect.

Lord,

I believe you hear and answer my every plea. I trust that when I cannot see your hand, you are still faithfully working on my behalf. I am certain that someday I will look back and understand your actions, know that you did what was best, and rejoice in your goodness and foresight.

Amen.

Day 45

My Jesus
covers me with His righteousness,
hides me in the shadow of His wings,
and holds me safely in His hand.

Philippians 3:9
Psalm 63:7
Psalm 139:9-10

Day 46

My Jesus
refines me through adversity when I lean into Him, helps me trust Him to strengthen my character, and assures me that victory will come in His time.

Psalm 66:10
1 Peter 2:20
James 1:3

Day 47

My Jesus
keeps my mind grounded in truth
while He lifts my spirit to soar in
freedom, beauty, and praise.

Colossians 2:6-7
Galatians 5:1
Psalm 27:4

Day 48

My Jesus
faithfully shields my soul from harm as He renders powerless every voice of condemnation and every destructive tactic of the enemy.

Romans 8:1-2
2 Thessalonians 3:3
2 Timothy 4:18

Day 49

My Jesus
provides timely repose when my mind needs to reorient and my spirit yearns for renewal.

Lord,

I love that you know exactly what I need and when. I am grateful that you provide it faithfully. Thank you for times of refreshing that invigorate my spirit and reset my outlook. Thank you for generously supplying all I need.

Amen.

Day 50

My Jesus
took the nails meant for me, wrote my name on the palms of His hands, and engraved His promises upon my heart.

1 John 2:2
Isaiah 49:16a
2 Corinthians 1:20a

Day 51

My Jesus
is servant and king, sacrifice and high priest, gentle lamb and mighty warrior.

Acts 3:26

Hebrews 7:26-27

Revelation 17:14

Day 52

My Jesus
covers my sin with His righteousness, cancels my guilt through His forgiveness, and by His unsurpassed power releases me from captivity.

Psalm 32:1
Colossians 2:13-14
Luke 4:17-20

Day 53

My Jesus
is hope for the hopeless, peace for the
troubled, and light for those living in darkness.

Isaiah 57:10
John 14:27
Matthew 4:16

Day 54

My Jesus
redeems me from my past mistakes,
carries me in my present, and assures
me that my future abounds with mercy,
love, and power from on high.

Lord,

I am humbly grateful that my past is forgiven by your boundless mercy, my present is infused with profound love, and my future is secure in your omnipotent hand. There is no place I would rather be than held in your mercy, love, and omnipotence.

Amen.

Day 55

My Jesus
marvelously makes me fearless, doubtless, and free by casting out fear, driving away doubt, and delivering me from strongholds.

1 John 4:18
Luke 24:36-49
2 Corinthians 10:3-4

Day 56

My Jesus
holds me guiltless for my sin, protects me from the enemy, and compassionately advocates for me before the Holy God.

Hebrews 9:15
1 Peter 1:3-5
1 John 2:1

Day 57

My Jesus
wants me to know the power of His presence, the peace of His forgiveness, and the reality of heaven so that I will live courageously, victoriously, and full of hope.

Romans 8:37-39
Job 19:25-27a
Joshua 1:9

Day 58

My Jesus
is the master of miraculous transformation,
restoration, and reconciliation.

2 Corinthians 3:18
Revelation 21:5
Romans 5:10

Day 59

My Jesus
reveals the ground I have yielded to the enemy, restores what was stolen, and shields me from deception when I abide in Him.

Lord,

Open my eyes to see the enemy's insidious actions, to stand against deception in the power and truth of your word, and to trust you to guard my mind and soul as I walk with you. Thank you for your healing revelations, divine protection, and restorative power.

Amen.

Day 60

My Jesus
allows whatever trials are necessary in my life to strengthen my faith and teach me how to stay the course when I would rather quit.

1 Peter 1:6-7
Ephesians 3:16
James 1:12

Day 61

My Jesus

is my endurance for the long road, my strength for the heavy loads, and my imperishable hope in the glory that awaits me at the finish line.

Isaiah 57:10

Hebrews 12:3

Matthew 11:28-30

Day 62

My Jesus
has mercifully given me His righteousness
yet rewards me as if it were my own.

Philippians 3:8-9
2 Corinthians 5:21
2 Timothy 4:7-8

Day 63

My Jesus
overturns lifeless idols with His power, upends foolish philosophies with His wisdom, and overcomes the adversary's lies with His truth.

1 Samuel 5:1-5
Corinthians 1:19
John 8:31-32

Day 64

My Jesus
is present and powerful in both happiness and sorrow, speaking through each as He draws my heart to His.

Lord,

You have brought me happiness and you have allowed sorrow. Thank you for drawing my heart to yours through each, never withholding happiness nor wasting my pain but beautifully weaving together all the intricate threads of my life. Your power to do so is breathtaking.

Amen.

Day 65

My Jesus
performs innumerable and obvious works on my behalf, and when I attempt to comprehend all He does that I cannot see, His tender care and bountiful provision overwhelm me.

Psalm 57:2
Isaiah 65:24
Philippians 4:19

Day 66

My Jesus

exceeds every expectation of mercy, shatters every preconception of grace, surpasses every human expression of authentic love, and proves deficient every estimation of His power, for He is always more than we can fully grasp this side of eternity.

Psalm 57:10
2 Chronicles 6:18
Genesis 18:14a

Day 67

My Jesus
is heaven's glory, earth's hope,
and Satan's defeat.

John 1:14
Colossians 1:3-8
Colossians 2:15

Day 68

My Jesus
lights my way because He is light,
increases my faith because He is
faithful, and leads me safely through
the unknown because He knows all.

Psalm 119:105
John 8:12
1 Thessalonians 5:24

Day 69

My Jesus
kindles the flame of my wholehearted devotion through His unfailing love, unmatched power, and unshakeable truth.

Lord,

Your love has never failed me. Your power is like no other. Your truth is everlasting. I wonder how could I not remain devoted to you. But hold me fast, Lord Jesus, lest I be tempted to wander.

Amen.

Day 70

My Jesus
beheld through His eyes of wisdom and love all of my moments and days before He created the universe and breathed life into humanity.

Jeremiah 1:5a
Psalm 139:15-16
Romans 11:33

Day 71

My Jesus
weaves together abundance and drought, solace and pain, and joy and grief in an elaborate tapestry that ultimately displays His sovereign foresight, incomparable wisdom, and eternal purpose.

Romans 8:28
Isaiah 61:3
Isaiah 46:9-10

Day 72

My Jesus
lifts me up when I am discouraged, fills me up when I confess my emptiness, and holds me up when I cannot stand on my own.

Psalm 145:14
Psalm 63:1-5
2 Chronicles 16:9a

Day 73

My Jesus
teaches me that religion without the sinner's repentance, the Savior's resurrection, and redemption through His blood is pointless and powerless to save.

Luke 13:5
1 Corinthians 15:13-14
Ephesians 1:7-8

Day 74

My Jesus
causes His word to resonate like a holy whisper within me that echoes from heaven's throne room to guide, grow, and fill me with hope.

Lord,

You have drawn me into your word, and you have caused it to sink deeply into my soul. I hear your words of encouragement replaying in my spirit. I hear your guidance speaking to my mind. I revel in the hope that fills me because of your truth. Let me always hear, O Lord. And let me always follow.

Amen.

Day 75

My Jesus
convicts me to seek holiness even as
He declares me holy by His blood.

1 Peter 1:14-16
Romans 3:21-24
Hebrews 10:10

Day 76

My Jesus
spins the invisible threads that hold atoms together, suspend the stars in the heavens, and tether my heart to His.

Colossians 1:16-17
Galatians 4:6
Jeremiah 31:35

Day 77

My Jesus
transforms so miraculously that the new barely recognizes the old, and each day dawns with renewed awe and humble gratefulness for how He alone can change a person—heart, mind, and soul.

2 Corinthians 5:17
Ezekiel 36:26
Romans 12:2

Day 78

My Jesus
begins, sustains, and completes good works
in my life for the glory of His name.

Philippians 1:6
Psalm 3:5
Matthew 5:16

Day 79

My Jesus
thought of me and my sin as He agonized in the Garden, as He bore the cross upon His shredded back, and as the soldiers hammered the spikes into His hands and feet, and He stayed the course to follow the Father's plan of redemption.

Lord,

I am overcome by the realization that you know all things and thought of me and every other soul when you suffered our guilt and punishment. Thank you for giving your life for mine, for bringing me to salvation through your extravagant mercy, and for carrying out the Father's perfect plan.

Amen.

Day 80

My Jesus
fortifies me with His word, illuminates my path with His light, and through His power, accomplishes in me what is humanly impossible.

Jeremiah 15:16
Psalm 119:130
Luke 18:27

Day 81

My Jesus
impresses upon me that when I truly appreciate the price He paid to extend grace and mercy, I can stop keeping score and freely open my heart and hands to others.

1 Peter 1:18-19
1 Corinthians 7:23a
Matthew 10:8b

Day 82

My Jesus
helps me discern between what is worthy
and worthless, what is authentic and fake,
and what is truthful and deceptive.

Hosea 14:9
Psalm 119:37
1 Corinthians 2:15b

Day 83

My Jesus
is Lord over the past, present, and future,
and in His foreknowledge and goodness
works out His plan through and in
spite of humanly inalterable events.

Psalm 31:15a
Psalm 103:19
Job 42:2

Day 84

My Jesus inspires me to celebrate every sustaining heartbeat, each invigorating breath, and all the miraculous facets of creation my eyes can see.

Lord,

Thank you for every ray of sunshine, every birdsong, every sparkling dewdrop, and every rainbow after a storm. Thank you for every heartbeat, each breath of fresh air, and the miraculous workings of my eyes that allow me to see the intricacies of your stunning creation.

Amen.

Day 85

My Jesus
fills me with peace that comforts,
trust that conquers fear, and faith
that can move mountains.

2 Thessalonians 3:16
Psalm 27:3
Mark 11:23

Day 86

My Jesus
is holy, just, and perfect, and yet He forgives my confessed sin, is merciful toward me in my failures, and patiently cultivates growth in me as His child.

1 Samuel 2:2
Deuteronomy 32:4
2 Peter 3:9

Day 87

My Jesus
walks through the flames of adversity with me, treads upon the roiling waves of conflict to rescue me, and stands firmly as the immovable rock to which I cling through every trial and tempest.

Daniel 8:24-27
Mark 6:47-52
2 Samuel 22:2-3

Day 88

My Jesus
cleanses the unclean, fills the empty, and redeems the lost.

Ezekiel 36:25

Psalm 81:10

Titus 2:11-14

Day 89

My Jesus
hears every cross word, knows every unholy thought, sees every selfish heart, and yet loves His children deeply enough to continue His work of sanctification.

Lord,

I am humbled that you know everything about me and still love me, that your love is greater than my failures, and that your power to purify me overcomes my sin. May I continually surrender to your divine sculpting as you form me into your likeness.

Amen.

Day 90

My Jesus
makes His presence known through timely nudges of direction, gentle whispers of encouragement, and faithful confirmations of truth He has planted and nurtured deep within my soul.

Psalm 37:23
Psalm 28:7
Proverbs 16:9

Day 91

My Jesus
is the living word who steeps the deepest parts
of my soul in His consuming love, gathers
my scattered thoughts and aligns them
with His wisdom, and overflows my heart
with peace that supplants earthly unrest.

Ephesians 3:14-19
James 1:5
Philippians 4:6-7

Day 92

My Jesus
pours out blessings that fulfill the fervent cries of my heart, the lofty aspirations of my mind, and the sacred yearnings of my soul.

Psalm 16:6
Psalm 18:6
Psalm 37:4

Day 93

My Jesus
mercifully bore my sin and powerfully bears my burdens, freeing my soul to bask in His mercy, unencumbered by guilt and cares.

1 Peter 2:24
Psalm 68:19
Psalm 119:45

Day 94

My Jesus
provides for every need, restores the lost hope, and heals the wounded spirit of every person who surrenders to Him.

Lord,

I know that the cattle on a thousand hills belong to you, and since you own everything, you provide everything I need. I trust that you know and can heal every hurt I have endured. Thank you for continuing to restore my hope and seal every fissure of my wounded spirit.

Amen.

Day 95

My Jesus
is mightier than a cruel cross, certain death, and a sealed grave.

Luke 24:6a
John 19:32-33
Matthew 27:66

Day 96

My Jesus
is the spotless lamb I could not afford, the eternal blessing I could never deserve, and the sweet forgiveness my soul was dying for.

Psalm 49:8a
Ephesians 2:1
1 John 1:9

Day 97

My Jesus
fashioned roadways through the wilderness of my heart and formed rivers in the parched desert of my spirit—healing, soothing, and refreshing.

Isaiah 43:19
Isaiah 57:15
Psalm 92:4

Day 98

My Jesus
makes me able to run in victory, walk in freedom, and live in peace.

1 Corinthians 15:57
Galatians 5:1a
Colossians 3:15

Day 99

My Jesus
calls me to new paths in different seasons and remains faithfully by my side to strengthen me and guide my every step.

Lord,

As I reflect on the seasons of my life, I see how you have been faithful and present through each. Thank you for the peace I have knowing that no matter what comes, you are always with me. Thank you for your strength and guidance each day in all my days. Help me be always in tune with your leading.

Amen.

Day 100

My Jesus
humbly stepped down from glory, willingly stepped into humanity, and lovingly stepped up to take my place on the cross.

Philippians 2:5-8
Romans 8:3
1 John 4:10

Day 101

My Jesus
never changes, never remembers
a forgiven sin, and never forgets
His promises to His people.

Malachi 3:6a
Hebrews 8:12
Deuteronomy 7:9

Day 102

My Jesus
is humility and majesty, mercy and justice,
and gentleness and tenacity perfected in
one infinitely wise and wondrous Savior.

Psalm 93:1
Deuteronomy 4:31
Isaiah 30:18

Day 103

My Jesus
helps me live an intentionally joyful life that spills over with His bountiful blessings.

Psalm 116:7
John 10:10
John 15:11

Day 104

My Jesus
masterfully arranges my every broken lament, my every pleading refrain, and my every sorrowful song into an eternal symphony of praise for His kindhearted care and restorative power.

Lord,

Your attentiveness to me is astonishing. That you have compassion for my every sorrow and rejoice with me through every victory draws my heart ever closer to yours. I look forward to joining in the anthems of praise that resound throughout eternity.

Amen.

Day 105

My Jesus
invited me to enter the holy of holies through the torn veil of His flesh so that I could be forgiven and live eternally with Him—all because of the costly exchange of His life for mine.

Mark 15:38
Ephesians 1:7-8
Psalm 49:8a

Day 106

My Jesus
is the infinite storehouse of all wisdom and reason, and He knows the answers to questions no human mind can construct.

Isaiah 46:10
Isaiah 40:25
Isaiah 40:28

Day 107

My Jesus
clothes me in His righteousness purely out of love, grace, and extraordinary generosity, and there is nothing I could ever do to deserve such a gift.

Psalm 31:19

Ephesians 1:6

Romans 5:17

Day 108

My Jesus
teaches me that should worldly treasures be stripped away, His everlasting truth, eternal promises, and enduring love remain.

Isaiah 40:8
Psalm 119:160
Psalm 103:17

Day 109

My Jesus
forgives, justifies, and redeems every sinner who believes, confesses, and repents.

Lord,

Thank you for forgiving me. Thank you for justifying me, for making it as if I had never sinned. Thank you for redeeming me by trading your life for mine. My mind cannot grasp your mercy, but I understand that it is only because of mercy that I believe in your name and have confessed and repented of my sins. Thank you from the depths of my grateful, rescued heart.

Amen.

Day 110

My Jesus
is the only name that imparts power,
peace, and provision when spoken in faith
and reverence from a repentant heart.

Philippians 2:9-11
Ephesians 1:18-21
Ephesians 2:14

Day 111

My Jesus
cleansed me, declared me righteous, and victoriously rescued me from the evil one when He paid my ransom with His blood.

John 1:7
Colossians 1:13-14
1 Timothy 2:5

Day 112

My Jesus

steps into situations that are all wrong and sets them right, walks into lives that are wrecked and transforms them, and enters sin-blackened hearts and makes them white as snow.

John 8:1-11
Luke 8:26-35
Isaiah 1:18

Day 113

My Jesus
gives me courage to face the storm,
carries me through the storm, and
transforms me by the storm.

John 16:33
Isaiah 46:4
1 Peter 1:6-7

Day 114

My Jesus
awakens my mind with truth, enlivens
my senses to discern His works, and
deepens my gratitude for His love
by blessing me beyond measure.

Lord,

I am grateful that your presence centers me in bright, pure light that illuminates my mind with truth. I am fascinated by how your spirit expands mine, igniting understanding and discernment. And I am in awe of your love that surrounds me with favor and showers me with blessings. My heart overflows.

Amen.

Day 115

My Jesus
is most assuredly returning someday to judge the earth and take His people home.

Psalm 98:9
1 Thessalonians 4:16-17
1 John 2:25

Day 116

My Jesus
is the almighty deliverer, faithful sustainer,
and trustworthy keeper of my soul.

Psalm 144:2

Psalm 3:5

Psalm 121:5-7

Day 117

My Jesus
holds me near and shields me from deception,
keeping me on His bright path where lies
are exposed in the light of His truth.

John 8:32
John 1:4-5
Psalm 36:9

Day 118

My Jesus
is the only remedy for deceived hearts that believe truth is relative, morals are to be ridiculed, and the temporal is of greater importance than the eternal.

Matthew 24:35
2 Peter 3:3
Matthew 6:20

Day 119

My Jesus
empowers me to walk in faith rather than fear, to rely on truth rather than feelings, and to depend on His strength rather than my own.

Lord,

Thank you for reminding me that faith vanquishes fear. Thank you for your truth that is the unchanging, solid foundation I can depend on. And thank you that when I come to the end of my own strength, in your strength I can persevere.

Amen.

Day 120

My Jesus
broke every chain, destroyed every stronghold, and freed me from every fetter that shackled me to sin, and I need only to trust in His deliverance.

2 Corinthians 10:4
Isaiah 58:6
Psalm 107:14

Day 121

My Jesus
displays His creative power through both microscope and telescope, and His majestic presence miraculously reverberates in His unseen works.

Colossians 1:16
Psalm 19:1
Colossians 1:26-27

Day 122

My Jesus
assures me that I need not fear bad news but trust instead that I am secure in His infinite knowledge, matchless wisdom, and profound love.

Psalm 112:6b-7
Colossians 2:2b-3
Romans 5:8

Day 123

My Jesus
confounded the wise, disarmed the enemy, and defeated death when He humbly lowered Himself into a manger, sacrificially stretched Himself out on the cross, and victoriously walked out of the tomb.

Colossians 2:15
Revelation 1:17-18
John 10:17-18

Day 124

My Jesus
held me in His heart when He held Himself to the cross, and now He holds my heart in His hands where it is forever safe from harm.

Lord,

I am filled with gratefulness when I consider that you held yourself to that cross for me when you could have stopped it all at any moment. To also know that this very moment— and for all my moments—you hold my heart safely in your hands gives me comfort beyond words. Thank you.

Amen.

Day 125

My Jesus
will one day judge the guilty, reward the righteous, and avenge the wrongly accused.

Nahum 1:2-3
Psalm 98:9
Revelation 22:12

Day 126

My Jesus
is the only source of true freedom,
the kind of soul-deep freedom that
transcends the machinations of man and
overpowers the schemes of the enemy.

John 8:36
Psalm 47:8
Psalm 37:7-9

Day 127

My Jesus
miraculously formed my body and soul,
faithfully supplies my every breath, and
will wondrously hold me together forever.

Psalm 139:13
Job 12:9-10
Colossians 1:17

Day 128

My Jesus
saves the reprehensible, heals the irreparable, and loves the unlovable.

Mark 3:1-5
Mark 10:27
Mark 1:40-42

Day 129

My Jesus
is never too busy to hear my need,
never mistaken about what I need, and
never late in meeting my need.

Lord,

I know that because you are all powerful and all knowing, you hear every need of every heart, you never make a mistake, and you are always on time. No matter how my circumstances sometimes seem to contradict these facts, they are still true, and you always and abundantly fulfill my every need. Thank you.

Amen.

Day 130

My Jesus
convicts me, not to drown me in the mire of guilt and shame, but to rescue me that I may enjoy sweet freedom—unfettered, unburdened, and uncondemned.

Psalm 3:3
John 3:17
Psalm 34:22

Day 131

My Jesus

provides rules, not to keep me in a cage, but to free me to live within healthy and safe boundaries.

Psalm 119:45
Deuteronomy 5:33
Psalm 119:32

Day 132

My Jesus
brings life through death, beauty from despair, and life-giving water to the heart's barren places.

Romans 6:4
Ecclesiastes 3:11a
John 4:13-14

Day 133

My Jesus
blesses me with ever-increasing faith,
envelops me in ever-abiding peace, and
immerses me in everlasting love.

Colossians 2:6-7
Philippians 4:5b-7
Psalm 136

Day 134

My Jesus
is esteemed by the humble mind,
revered by the repentant heart, and
adored by the redeemed soul.

Lord,

How rightfully you are esteemed by the humble, by those who understand your authority as Lord and King. How glorified you are by those who behold a glimpse of your holiness and genuinely repent. And oh, how adored you are by those whose souls you have redeemed at great cost! Lord, in your mercy and continual grace, keep me always in this holy assembly.

Amen.

Day 135

My Jesus
has a voice that spoke the universe into existence, a name that incites fear in the enemy, and a heart that overflows with tenderness for His beloved.

Psalm 33:9
James 2:19
Luke 1:76-79

Day 136

My Jesus
is not one path among many paths
but the only path that leads to
salvation, peace, and eternal life.

John 14:6
Matthew 7:13-14
John 10:9

Day 137

My Jesus
blesses me with abundant grace, fathomless mercy, and eternal redemption—all undeserved, unearned, and unending.

Ephesians 1:7-8a
1 Peter 1:3
Psalm 103:17

Day 138

My Jesus
holds all of my if-onlys, what-ifs, and whys
securely in His omniscience and omnipotence
and assures me all will be well in His time.

Psalm 147:5
Matthew 10:30-31
Matthew 28:18

Day 139

My Jesus
teaches me that man's knowledge without God's wisdom is empty, vain, and useless.

Lord,

Thank you for showing me that seeking and receiving your wisdom helps me know what to do with the knowledge I have. Without your wisdom I would be simply a walking dictionary or encyclopedia of no spiritual use to anyone. Help me continue to grow in wisdom and knowledge of truth and to compassionately share them with others.

Amen.

Day 140

My Jesus
searches my heart to convict me,
regenerates my mind to conform me,
and fills my soul to complete me.

Jeremiah 17:10
Revelation 3:19
Psalm 73:24

Day 141

My Jesus
gives me countless reasons to be thankful when I look outward to admire creation resplendent with His glory, upward to focus on the wonder of the eternal, and inward to marvel at how He has brought my soul to life.

Nehemiah 9:6
Psalm 145:13
John 5:24

Day 142

My Jesus
has the power to heal and transform
what is into what should be.

Matthew 4:24
Joel 2:25-26
Romans 4:17

Day 143

My Jesus
speaks hope into my discouragement, strength into my weakness, and calm into my chaos.

Romans 15:4
2 Corinthians 12:9
Psalm 107:28-30

Day 144

My Jesus
exchanges dejection for a glad heart, indifference for a compassionate spirit, anxiety for a tranquil soul, and confusion for a mind enlightened by godly wisdom.

Lord,

I know this to be true because I witness it in my life. Does it mean that I am never dejected or indifferent? That I am never anxious or confused? No. It means that when I do find myself in those valleys, I trust you to pour out gladness, compassion, tranquility, and wisdom to lift me up, reset my outlook, and refocus my thoughts. Thank you.

Amen.

Day 145

My Jesus
reaches down into the pit of despair to lift the hopeless ones and anchor them firmly in unshakable faith, liberating forgiveness, and heartening fellowship.

Isaiah 28:16
2 Corinthians 3:17
1 John 1:7

Day 146

My Jesus
compassionately shares my grief over earthly losses, comforts as only He can, and wondrously promises no tears in heaven.

John 11:33-35
Isaiah 53:4
Revelation 21:4

Day 147

My Jesus
teaches me of grace when He helps me learn from the consequences of my mistakes, mercifully alters the consequences, or powerfully rescues me from the consequences.

Psalm 51:17
Psalm 25:15
Psalm 103:10

Day 148

My Jesus
arms me for battle with the weapon of His word, dispatches heaven's hosts to go before me, and infuses me with courage far beyond myself.

Ephesians 6:17
Psalm 91:11-12
Psalm 56:3-4

Day 149

My Jesus
is my safe place to pour out my heart as I
confess all my sins and lay down every burden.

Lord,

Because you know everything about me and love me still, I know that in you I always have a safe place. I am ever grateful that confessing my sins to you brings freedom rather than condemnation and that surrendering every burden to your capable hands sets me free.

Amen.

Day 150

My Jesus
masterfully fashioned the planets, skillfully scattered the stars in the heavens, and continually paints an ever-changing display of His glory across the sky.

Genesis 1:18
Colossians 1:16
Psalm 19:1

Day 151

My Jesus
atoned for my sin and appeased God's wrath by shedding His redeeming blood, satisfying the divine requirement for a spotless sacrifice.

1 John 1:2
Hebrews 9:11-12
Romans 3:21-26

Day 152

My Jesus
offers genuine joy, serenity, and contentment in place of superficial happiness, anxious restlessness, and angry discontent.

1 Peter 1:8
Psalm 107:6
Philippians 4:11

Day 153

My Jesus
demonstrates His incomparable power
when I humbly admit my weakness,
lack of knowledge, and inability
to alter my circumstances.

Ephesians 1:18-21
Psalm 6:2-3, 9-10
Psalm 73:21-24

Day 154

My Jesus
daily pours out mercy so that each morning when I awake, I know He has already supplied what I need to face the day.

Lord,

Thank you for this comfort that you always know what I will need in each moment and that your provision is perfect and plentiful. Please Lord, when I forget, remind me. When I doubt, forgive me. And when I feel too weak to face the day, show me that your strength is greater than I could ever need.

Amen.

Day 155

My Jesus
is heaven's glorious victor over hate, death, and despair because He is love incarnate, life everlasting, and hope eternal.

Luke 6:27-29
John 1:4-5
1 Corinthians 15:54-55

Day 156

My Jesus
is rightfully acknowledged as Savior, Lord, and King through sincere worship, humble obedience, and solemn submission to His sovereignty.

John 4:24-26
1 Peter 1:2
Jeremiah 32:17

Day 157

My Jesus
helps me guard my mouth, quiet my heart, and focus my mind to honor Him, enjoy His peace, and live fully committed to Him each moment.

Psalm 141:3
Philippians 4:4-9
Ephesians 5:15-16

Day 158

My Jesus
instills heavenly peace that overcomes worry,
supernatural power that presses on through
afflictions, and blessed solace that heals
the most painful wounds of the heart.

James 1:12
Luke 12:31-32
Malachi 4:2

Day 159

My Jesus
provides what I need for each situation and moment, and He walks with me through difficulties I could not have imagined.

Lord,

I know that you know all things, but sometimes when I face a difficult trial, what my mind knows is overshadowed by what my heart feels. So please continue to remind me that nothing surprises you and nothing comes my way that is not filtered through your omnipotent love and perfect provision.

Amen.

Day 160

My Jesus
is the divine regeneration of the sin-tainted mind, the gentle repair of the sin-wounded heart, and the victorious resurrection of the sin-deadened soul.

Titus 3:5-7
Psalm 147:3
1 Corinthians 15:22

Day 161

My Jesus
saw the sinner I was and knew the redeemed child I could be through His forgiveness, and He offered it freely.

Psalm 33:13-15
Psalm 139:1-2
Isaiah 55:1

Day 162

My Jesus
shed blood that is pure enough,
extends grace that is broad enough,
and supplies mercy that is deep enough
to redeem every repentant sinner.

Romans 5:20-21
Hebrews 10:22
1 Timothy 1:12-16

Day 163

My Jesus
settles the restless heart, satisfies the searching heart, and emboldens the timid heart.

Psalm 46:10
Jeremiah 29:13
2 Timothy 1:7

Day 164

My Jesus
teaches me that viewing my faith as a fact instead of a feeling strengthens my faith and aligns my feelings with scriptural truth.

Lord,

Thank you that as I exercise my faith by standing on the solid ground of your word rather than on the shifting sand of my feelings, you increase my faith and help my feelings align with your truth. May it ever be so, in Jesus' name.

Amen.

Day 165

My Jesus
grounds me in truth, walks with me in power, and raises me up to new life through His word, His Spirit, and His resurrection.

Matthew 7:24-25
2 Peter 1:3
Romans 6:4

Day 166

My Jesus
is the omnipotent sustainer of the universe,
the inextinguishable light of the world,
and the comforting hope of the nations.

Colossians 1:17
John 8:12
Matthew 12:21

Day 167

My Jesus
breathed the heavens into existence,
breathed life into humanity, and breathes
joy and peace into every surrendered soul.

Psalm 33:6
Genesis 2:7
Romans 15:13

Day 168

My Jesus
washed the feet of His betrayer, interceded
for those who crucified Him, and restored
the one who denied Him because He
is humble, merciful, and forgiving.

John 13:5-12
Luke 23:33-34
John 21:15-19

Day 169

My Jesus
has been gracious to me in my ignorance and merciful to me in my hypocrisy, and in my rebellion has patiently but persistently drawn me to Himself with abiding love.

Lord,

If not for the grace and mercy you have extended to me, I would be suffocated by guilt and shame. What a heavy burden your love has removed from my soul. What lightness of spirit and freedom from condemnation I enjoy because of your graciousness to me. Thank you.

Amen.

Day 170

My Jesus
is heaven's perfect Lamb who was tempted yet pure, tried yet true, and crucified yet magnificently victorious.

John 1:29
Hebrews 4:15
Revelation 1:17-18

Day 171

My Jesus
promises to make a way for me through the difficult and impossible, and He whispers into my wondering and worrying that He always keeps His promises.

Luke 18:27
Isaiah 43:19
Matthew 6:25-26

Day 172

My Jesus
arrayed the constellations like glittering ornaments, uniquely designed the earth to support life and display His beauty, and with incomprehensible power and stunning creativity, fashioned the intricate details of every creature.

Isaiah 40:26
Romans 1:20
Genesis Chapter 1

Day 173

My Jesus
mercifully changes mockers into worshippers, doubters into believers, and the faithless into the faithful because He who created the soul has the power to redeem it, transform it, and set it free.

Acts 7:58-8:3
John 20:24-29
Galatians 1:23-24

Day 174

My Jesus
works mightily in the one who humbly seeks wisdom and courage and is willing to follow Him no matter the cost.

Lord,

I need your wisdom to guide me. I need your courage to take the steps in the direction you want me to go. Help me trust you to lead and strengthen me, and help me always to seek your wisdom and courage so that I may daily walk in faith—no matter the cost.

Amen.

Day 175

My Jesus
remains strong in my weakness and helps me trust Him when my feelings fluctuate, troubles multiply, and the enemy whispers doubt.

Hebrews 6:19
John 16:33
Luke 17:6

Day 176

My Jesus
is mercy that is new every morning,
forgiveness that has no memory, and
peace that transcends the temporal.

Lamentations 3:22-23
Isaiah 43:25
2 Corinthians 4:17-18

Day 177

My Jesus
reminds me that worry, anxiety, and fear are emotions counter-productive to faith and hold no sway over the redeemed child of the living God.

Philippians 4:6-7
Psalm 118:6
2 Corinthians 10:3-6

Day 178

My Jesus
shaped the mountains and valleys, drew the boundary lines for the oceans, and spun the earth into a perfectly synced orbit around a sphere of hot plasma that supports life on our magnificently unique planet.

Psalm 65:6
Job 38:8-11
Genesis 1:14-19

Day 179

My Jesus

knows my every sin but still requires me to confess, knows everything I need but still wants me to ask, and has the power to accomplish whatever He wishes but chooses to involve me in His kingdom work.

Lord,

I understand that it is for my benefit— for the health of my soul and for the tearing down of walls between you and me—that you want me to confess and repent. Thank you for loving me enough to nurture a relationship with me, for providing for my needs, and for allowing me to participate in your plan.

Amen.

Day 180

My Jesus
sanctifies my mind as He draws me to holiness, assures me that my soul is hidden in His righteousness, and heartens my spirit as He walks me home.

1 Corinthians 2:16b
Romans 4:7-8
Philippians 3:9

Day 181

My Jesus

causes me to tremble at His holiness, to wonder how He could die in my place, and to rejoice that He freed me from the burden of sin and shame.

Exodus 15:11
2 Corinthians 5:21
Romans 8:1-2

Day 182

My Jesus
is gentle with me when I do not understand His actions, and He comforts me with patient reminders that His love is perfect and sufficient.

Proverbs 3:5-6
2 Peter 3:9
2 Corinthians 12:9

Day 183

My Jesus
is my healing song in sorrow, my strengthening praise through times of testing, and my certain victory over defeat.

Isaiah 61:3
Psalm 40:2-3
1 John 5:4

Day 184

My Jesus
is the peace that encompasses me,
the confidence that inspires me,
and the fortitude that equips me to
remain faithful and finish well.

Lord,

The certainty of your love and power, the confidence and peace of knowing you hold my life in the palm of your hand, and the courage you miraculously bestow are gifts of indescribable value to me. Because of your good gifts and perfect provision, I can press on. Thank you.

Amen.

Day 185

My Jesus
set me free from bondage to sin, and because He broke my chains, my soul is liberated and my heart sings freedom's anthem of amazing grace.

Romans 8:2
Psalm 119:45
Galatians 5:1

Day 186

My Jesus
knows me better than I know myself, understands my needs beyond what I can comprehend, and compassionately intercedes for me before the Father.

Psalm 139:3
Matthew 6:8
Romans 8:34

Day 187

My Jesus
appointed the day of my birth, holds my days and years in His hands, and has planned for the moment I will take my first breath in heaven.

Psalm 139:16
Psalm 31:15a
Hebrews 9:27

Day 188

My Jesus
renews my mind, refreshes my spirit, and comforts my heart in a world that seeks to confuse, wear down, and wound.

Romans 12:2
Jeremiah 31:25
2 Corinthians 1:3

Day 189

My Jesus
gently beckons to wandering hearts inviting them to His limitless wisdom, His comforting truth, and His always open arms.

Lord,

When I truly consider your fathomless wisdom, mercy, and grace, I wonder how I could ever wander from your side. But when I do, you welcome me back to your open arms where I experience the indescribable peace of being held by the lover of my soul. Hold me ever closer, sweet Jesus.

Amen.

Day 190

My Jesus
perfects His will in my life through His knowledge, power, and absolute command of time and events.

Hebrews 12:20-21
Psalm 57:2
Psalm 119:91b

Day 191

My Jesus
is the only sure and solid foothold
for this life of shifting circumstances
and uncertain outcomes.

Psalm 26:12
Isaiah 54:10
Luke 6:46-49

Day 192

My Jesus
at once commands the operation of the far reaches of the universe while showing compassionate care for the intricate workings of my heart.

Hebrews 11:3
James 5:11
Acts 15:8

Day 193

My Jesus
desires relationship, not religion, and offers freedom, not bondage, for He is a chain breaker, not a chain maker.

Psalm 51:16-17
Galatians 4:3-5
Acts 12:7

Day 194

My Jesus
is gloriously just, wholly loving, and unfathomably patient, yet in due time He will recompense His enemies and restore to the righteous infinitely more than has been lost.

Lord,

I am thankful that you are patient and loving. I am also thankful that you are just and that one day you will right all wrongs and avenge your enemies. I look forward to the moment when you wipe away the tears of your beloved ones and fill every empty place. My earthbound mind cannot imagine such peace and utter joy. But oh, how I long to experience it.

Amen.

Day 195

My Jesus
calms, refreshes, and strengthens me
when I trust in His transcendent serenity,
supernatural sustenance, and matchless power.

Psalm 91:1
Jeremiah 31:25
Ephesians 1:19

Day 196

My Jesus
is my always faithful defender, stalwart shield, and triumphant warrior who fights my battles, defending me in power and faithfulness.

Colossians 2:15
Deuteronomy 20:4
Psalm 89:8

Day 197

My Jesus
delivered me from shame by taking all of it upon Himself, blessedly turning my heart toward His and changing me forever.

2 Corinthians 5:17
Ezekiel 36:26
Romans 6:4

Day 198

My Jesus
invites me to trust in His presence, dwell in His peace, and walk in His power.

Matthew 28:20b
Philippians 4:4-7
Luke 10:19

Day 199

My Jesus
fascinates my mind more than the most profound book, tugs at my heart like a velvet cord gently drawing me to Himself, and soothes my soul like a peaceful, cleansing current.

Lord,

When I spend time with you by reading your word, I am intrigued, empowered, and enlightened. Your word transforms my mind and ignites my soul while it also cleanses, calms, and refreshes every part of me. Thank you that through the power of your Spirit, such shall always be true.

Amen.

Day 200

My Jesus
submits to neither the will of man nor of nations but answers the prayers of humble and righteous hearts as He sovereignly carries out His plan.

Ezekiel 12:28
Proverbs 15:29
Jeremiah 18:7-10

Day 201

My Jesus
could have summoned the host of heaven to destroy the evil ones and deliver Himself from death on the cross, yet because of love, He finished what He came to do.

Matthew 26:53-54
Romans 5:8
John 15:12-13

Day 202

My Jesus
strengthens me for the task at hand, prepares me for what is ahead even when I do not realize it, and faithfully walks with me through it all.

Psalm 138:3
2 Peter 1:2-3
Isaiah 43:2

Day 203

My Jesus
perfectly exhibits the beauty of humility,
the supremacy of divine wisdom, and the
sacrificial nature of authentic love.

Matthew 11:29
Revelation 5:12
Romans 5:8

Day 204

My Jesus
holds me tightly when the enemy attempts to pull me down, brings forth His praises when the enemy tries to silence me, and rejoices with me in victory when the enemy flees in defeat.

Lord,

Thank you for always holding on to me, especially when the enemy tugs at my mind and tries to sap my strength. Thank you for your protective power and deliverance. Thank you for every victory when your light and truth chase away the darkness. My soul overflows with praise and thanksgiving.

Amen.

Day 205

My Jesus
is the bridge that spans the chasm
between my unrighteousness and
the most high and holy God.

1 Peter 3:18
Isaiah 64:6
1 Peter 1:15-16

Day 206

My Jesus
lives in me, and that is the remarkable mystery, mercy, and majesty of the gospel.

Colossians 1:24-27
1 Corinthians 3:16
2 Peter 1:4

Day 207

My Jesus
gave me life when I was dead in sin, extended mercy when I was destined for judgment, and shined His light upon me when I was stumbling in darkness.

Ephesians 2:1-3
James 2:12b
Colossians 1:13-14

Page 208

My Jesus
has established my way before me,
and I need only to walk in it faithfully,
prayerfully, and expectantly.

Psalm 40:2
Psalm 119:110
Psalm 5:3

Day 209

My Jesus
loves me more thoroughly than my mind can comprehend, and my heart and soul crave His love and receive it joyfully.

Lord,

Your love heals my heart and soul and fills me with inexpressible joy. Even though words cannot describe the depth of your love, when I look to the cross I see there your sacrifice for me and begin to understand love. I hear it calling me, flowing from your heart, and I step into the divine deluge where I am immersed in pure, holy love.

Amen.

Day 210

My Jesus
rains nourishment into my soul like manna from heaven that I gather and savor, trusting that it is always plentiful and timely.

Psalm 36:7-8
Isaiah 58:11
Psalm 13:6

Day 211

My Jesus
draws all people to Himself, showing them kindness and mercy they cannot understand or appreciate until He helps them grasp the magnitude of their sin and desperate need for salvation.

John 12:32
Luke 6:35
1 Corinthians 2:14

Day 212

My Jesus
grants me more than a second chance when I fail Him, for His grace is a continual chance to leave failure and its burden behind and begin anew.

John 1:6
Micah 7:18
Lamentations 3:22-23

Day 213

My Jesus
goes before me in power, walks alongside me in companionship, and carries me tenderly when I cannot walk on my own.

Isaiah 52:12
Isaiah 43:2
Isaiah 46:4

Day 214

My Jesus
relentlessly drew me to Himself
and thoroughly won my heart
with His unfathomable mercy
and extravagant kindness.

Lord,

Your extraordinary kindness and tenderhearted mercy speak healing and hope to my soul. Because you never give up on me and because you have set me free from guilt and shame, my heart and my life are yours forever.

Amen.

Day 215

My Jesus
ministers to the angry heart to soothe it, exposes the hard heart to warn of judgment, and convicts the sinful heart to sanctify it and set it free.

Romans 2:5-6
2 Corinthians 7:9-10
Psalm 32:5-7

Day 216

My Jesus
is the source of all wisdom, and He generously
gives it to all who ask in humility and faith.

James 1:5-6
Proverbs 11:2
Romans 11:23

Day 217

My Jesus
is a many-faceted, priceless gem
of immeasurable value, matchless
splendor, and sparkling brilliance that
fills my life with beauty and light.

Matthew 13:45
Psalm 71:8
2 Corinthians 4:6

Day 218

My Jesus
declares rebirth from the manger, forgiveness from the cross, eternal life from the empty tomb, and everlasting hope from His heart to mine.

Matthew 1:23
1 Corinthians 15:17
Colossians 1:5

Day 219

My Jesus
is the gift of heaven whose infant cry, dying words, and resurrected voice resound through the ages with the hope-filled message that God Himself came to dwell with us, deliver us, and give us life.

Lord,

I can hardly fathom that you left the glory of heaven to come to us, to live among us and suffer for our sin. Thank you for coming down to make a way for us to come to you. Thank you for your sacrifice and deliverance, and thank you for the gifts of life and hope.

Amen.

Day 220

My Jesus
assures me that I can unequivocally trust in His ever-present and lavish grace toward me rather than wish, worry, or wonder if I will receive it.

1 John 3:19-20
Ephesians 1:15-21
1 John 5:13

Day 221

My Jesus
brings peace in panic, calm in conflict,
and joy in the midst of heartache.

Psalm 107:28-29

Psalm 73:26

Psalm 138:7

Day 222

My Jesus
saved me though I was unworthy, loved me though I was unlovable, and forgave me though I was unforgivable because He is immeasurably gracious, loving, and merciful.

Romans 5:8
1 Corinthians 6:9-11
Psalm 111:4

Day 223

My Jesus
loves me for the Bible, the cross, and the Holy Spirit within me tell me it is so.

Ephesians 5:2
Hebrews 7:26-27
Romans 5:5

Day 224

My Jesus
keeps me always in His heart, securely in His arms, and forever on His mind.

Lord,

When I remember that you think of every person at every moment and hold on to every person at every moment, I am utterly astonished. Such knowledge soothes my spirit, brings me peace of mind, and calms my soul. I truly have nothing to fear. Thank you.

Amen.

Day 225

My Jesus
never gets sidetracked, never loses His focus, and forgets nothing except what He chooses to for mercy's sake.

Isaiah 55:11

Psalm 32:8

Isaiah 43:25

Day 226

My Jesus
is the pinnacle of power, the deepest well of mercy, and the richest treasure of wisdom and truth.

Isaiah 44:7-8
Colossians 2:1-3
Psalm 103:17

Day 227

My Jesus
is love I cannot diminish, mercy I cannot exhaust, and forgiveness I cannot erase.

1 John 4:16
Luke 6:36
John 1:16

Day 228

My Jesus
never agonizes over any situation nor
wonders how He will solve any problem
because He has complete knowledge
of every detail and scenario.

Isaiah 25:1
Hebrews 4:13
Isaiah 46:9-10

Day 229

My Jesus
gently holds the grief-stricken heart as He seals up every rift with His consuming love and fills to overflowing the empty, aching places with eternal hope.

Lord,

I have experienced your comfort in grief, and I have witnessed it in others as you have carried them through the pain of loss. The hope we receive and your love that buoys us up amid heart-wrenching sorrow set your people apart from the world and set you apart as the one and only comforter of our souls. Thank you.

Amen.

Day 230

My Jesus
remarkably changed my heart, mind, and life, and when I remember what I once was, I am awed by His transforming power and deeply grateful for His sweet mercy.

2 Corinthians 5:17
2 Corinthians 3:18
Psalm 18:19

Day 231

My Jesus
made everything from nothing by speaking
it all into being, and He can indeed
work miraculously in every situation.

Genesis 1
Psalm 33:6
Ephesians 1:21

Day 232

My Jesus
perfectly perceives my needs in every moment and is always willing and able to do infinitely more on my behalf than I am capable of asking.

Ephesians 3:20-21
Psalm 147:5
Matthew 6:8

Day 233

My Jesus
surrounds me with His favor,
astounds me with His goodness, and
humbles me with His holiness.

Psalm 147:11
Psalm 34:8
1 Peter 1:15-16

Day 234

My Jesus
is the sinless One crushed by my sin, the guiltless One sacrificed for me as a guilt offering, and the righteous One who covers me with His righteousness.

Lord,

How do I thank you for becoming sin for me, for paying my debt, and for giving me your righteousness? Mere words cannot express my gratefulness. So, by your grace, I live for you, and in your strength, I honor you in all I do. May my life be a beacon of your love shining brightly upon those around me.

Amen.

Day 235

My Jesus
is so powerful, majestic, and mighty that even the reverent whisper of His beautiful name destroys strongholds, sets captives free, and renders the enemy powerless.

Psalm 8:1
Philippians 2:10
Luke 10:17-19

Day 236

My Jesus

recorded for us a grand story that seems too wonderful to be true, is too evidential to be false, and is too beautiful to have been written by mere men.

1 Peter 1:3-5
1 Corinthians 15:4-6
2 Timothy 3:16-17

Day 237

My Jesus
captures my thoughts, filters my words, and guides my actions when I abide in His truth and surrender my will to His.

Psalm 141:3
Psalm 119:133
James 4:7

Day 238

My Jesus
makes every trial I endure count for something beautiful and sanctifying in my life and for His kingdom.

2 Corinthians 8:1-2
James 1:2-4
Psalm 66:10

Day 239

My Jesus
brings clarity amid confusion, fashions healing from brokenness, and offers redemption instead of condemnation.

Lord,

Thank you for helping me understand that many troubling behaviors—my own and others'—stem from brokenness. Help me offer forgiveness and grace rather than condemnation, both to myself and to others. And thank you for doing the same for me.

Amen.

Day 240

My Jesus
brings the faithful believer, though weary
and battle-worn, to promised victory,
jubilant celebration, and eternal reward.

Galatians 6:9
Revelation 3:21
Revelation 19:7-9

Day 241

My Jesus
guides my heart to help me understand His word, He whispers truth to my mind to defeat deception, and He rejoices with me when His fire ignites yet another piece of my soul.

Hebrews 4:12
Psalm 19:7-8
Luke 24:45

Day 242

My Jesus
knows my heart more deeply than I do,
understands precisely what I need, and
answers my prayers better than I pray them.

>Jeremiah 12:3a
>Philippians 4:19
>Romans 8:26-27

Day 243

My Jesus
knows what is secreted away behind the walls of every heart, He understands every trauma and bitterness, and He desires to bring all of it into the light so He can heal it.

Psalm 44:2
Hebrews 4:15
Psalm 34:18

Day 244

My Jesus
shelters me when clouds of confusion spill their torrent, He vanquishes fear when it threatens to defeat me, and He walks with me through all the shadowed moments of the unknown.

Lord,

Thank you for safe shelter when confusion rains down and fear assails. Thank you for always abiding with me. Because you know all things, have all power, and do all things well, your presence continually reassures me that with you I can face whatever comes next.

Amen.

Day 245

My Jesus
strengthens in times of weakness,
encourages in times of disappointment,
and refreshes in times of drought.

2 Corinthians 12:10
Romans 15:5
Jeremiah 41:25

Day 246

My Jesus
is the central figure in a divine story that
is dramatic yet serene, mysterious yet
simple, and tragic yet triumphant.

1 Peter 1:20-21
1 Timothy 3:16
Matthew 20:18-19

Day 247

My Jesus
cannot be contained, restrained, or fully explained, yet He lowers Himself to reveal His character to those who seek Him in faith.

Psalm 97:9
Isaiah 14:27
Philippians 2:5-7

Day 248

My Jesus
settles every anxious heart, soothes every bitter heart, and mends every shattered heart placed in His hands.

2 Corinthians 7:6
Psalm 139:23-24
Psalm 30:2

Day 249

My Jesus
is my lifeline in rough seas of doubt, my secure vessel who carries me through storms of despair, and my safe harbor in whom I rest from the tumultuous trials of life.

Lord,

Countless times you have gently counteracted my doubt with your faithfulness. You have helped me weather the storms of discouragement and despair, and you have given me sweet rest in the shelter of your wings where all is peace. Thank you.

Amen.

Day 250

My Jesus
commands me to heed His entire word, not just pick and choose which parts I consider true, convenient, or worthy of obedience.

James 1:23-25
Psalm 119:160
Psalm 119:11

Day 251

My Jesus
declares me saved, forgiven, and righteous by His blood, gloriously contradicting what the world, my flesh, and the enemy say I am.

1 Corinthians 1:18
Romans 5:1-2
Revelation 1:5b

Day 252

My Jesus
commands the unseen, performs the miraculous, and conquers the impossible.

Colossians 1:16
Hebrews 2:4
Matthew 19:26

Day 253

My Jesus
passionately pursues the lost,
gently comforts the wounded, and
lovingly fathers the fatherless.

1 Timothy 2:3-4
2 Corinthians 1:3-4
2 Corinthians 6:18

Day 254

My Jesus
does not define me by the enemy's attempts to entice, deceive, and destroy me but by the righteous One who lives in me.

Lord,

This world flaunts its sin and even desires to be labeled according to it. Thank you that who I am is defined by you and you alone, not by my sin or failures nor by other human beings. Thank you that your righteousness in me is the identity I desire and by your grace is who I am.

Amen.

Day 255

My Jesus
blessedly chooses mercy and forgiveness even though He has the right to remind me of my failures and to hold my sin against me.

Psalm 103:10-12
Numbers 9:31
Luke 6:36

Day 256

My Jesus
helps me guard my heart and mind,
and He zealously protects me from the
insidious subterfuge of this age.

Psalm 119:33-34
Psalm 19:7-11
Hebrews 13:9

Day 257

My Jesus
masterfully choreographs my moments, wisely directs my steps, and divinely orders my days to accomplish His will and assure me of His presence.

Isaiah 14:27
Isaiah 48:17
Psalm 46:7

Day 258

My Jesus
is not a genie in a bottle, a magician who waves a wand, nor a circus act who performs on cue but the almighty God who graciously hears and answers the prayers of righteous people.

Job 38-39
Acts 4:24
Psalm 116:2

Day 259

My Jesus
urges me to remember all the wonders He has performed so I will understand and trust in what He can do on my behalf and on behalf of those I love.

Lord,

Thank you for this reminder to remember. Bring to mind all the wonders you have done for me, for those I love, and for all of mankind. Replay for me your merciful and mighty acts so I remember your powerful intercession and goodness. Ever remind me, O Lord, of who you are and what you can do.

Amen.

Day 260

My Jesus
is the Savior whose heart overflows with unceasing love for His children, tender compassion for the broken ones, and joyful delight each time a soul receives His healing.

John 15:9
Matthew 14:14
Luke 15:3-7

Day 261

My Jesus
breaks the chains of spiritual oppression
so that every liberated captive experiences
genuine freedom of the soul.

Luke 4:18-19
Psalm 124:7-8
2 Corinthians 3:17

Day 262

My Jesus
assures me that because of His gift of eternal life, one day I will slip the bonds of earth and flesh and enjoy His glorious presence and power forever.

2 Corinthians 5:8
1 John 5:11
Jude 1:24-25

Day 263

My Jesus
promises mercy and grace enough for this moment and is abundantly prepared to supply what is needed in the next.

2 Corinthians 9:8
Exodus 34:6
Hebrews 4:16

Day 264

My Jesus
so captivates me that the more deeply I come to know Him, the more I want to know Him.

Lord,

I am truly enraptured by you. When I contemplate what I know about you today compared to what I knew about you a year or a decade ago, I am so grateful that you have drawn me to you and helped me learn and grow. Especially compelling is how I will never finish learning about you. Thank you that I never want to stop.

Amen.

Day 265

My Jesus
commands armies of angels I cannot see, ordains His works in ways I cannot fully know, and thinks wondrous thoughts I cannot comprehend.

Matthew 26:53
Ecclesiastes 11:5
Isaiah 55:8-9

Day 266

My Jesus
makes an undeniable difference in the repentant and surrendered life and grants radiant joy, inner peace, and sublime strength.

2 Corinthians 5:17
Galatians 5:22-23
Colossians 1:9-12

Day 267

My Jesus
reversed my death sentence at the cross, and by walking out of the grave, He gave me victory in this life and a glorious forever with Him in the next.

Philippians 4:13
2 Peter 1:10-11
2 Timothy 1:12

Day 268

My Jesus
is absolutely perfect yet tenderly approachable,
humanly indescribable yet supernaturally
knowable, and majestically enthroned on
high yet powerfully present with me.

Ephesians 3:11-12
Psalm 34:8
Colossians 3:1

Day 269

My Jesus,
who mightily commands the wind,
determines the paths of the stars, and calls
forth the flowers in their seasons, guards
and cherishes each of His children.

Lord,

It is great solace to witness your stunning power over and intricate care for your creation. From the seasons to the flowers to the stars, you command all of them while also loving and guarding the souls of those whose names are in your book. Hallelujah!

Amen.

Day 270

My Jesus
helps me step back and rest, refresh, and refocus when constant activity and distractions threaten to drain and discourage me.

Matthew 11:28
Matthew 4:18-19
Psalm 123:2

Day 271

My Jesus
speaks with a voice that is fearsome yet comforting, ethereal yet perceivable, and consuming yet life-giving to those with ears to hear.

Psalm 29:8
John 10:27
John 6:68

Day 272

My Jesus
helps me keep walking when the road is strewn with obstacles and keep climbing when the path is steep and twisting, and He faithfully safeguards me through every peril.

Romans 5:3-5
1 Samuel 2:9
Psalm 63:8

Day 273

My Jesus
delights my soul with wondrous mercy that removed my guilt, unchanging truth that anchors my mind, and enduring peace that carries me through every trial.

Psalm 84:2
Galatians 2:16
Hebrews 13:8

Day 274

My Jesus
endears Himself to me through my every remembrance of His forgiveness, my every awareness of His serenity, and His every generous provision for my needs.

Lord,

When I remember what I once was and how you have brought me thus far by your mercy and tenderness, my heart nearly bursts with gratefulness. Your forgiveness, peace, and provision free my soul to walk joyfully through this life while expectantly looking to the next with you.

Amen.

Day 275

My Jesus
convicts me to repent of every disobedient thought, word, and deed, submitting all to His holy authority and trusting in His compassionate forgiveness.

James 4:7a
2 Corinthians 10:3-5
Acts 3:19

Day 276

My Jesus
is more awesome, just, and holy than we dare to admit, but more patient, loving, and merciful than we can imagine.

Hebrews 10:31
Romans 2:4
Habakkuk 1:13a

Day 277

My Jesus
reminds me that no situation, mind, or heart is beyond the reach of His omnipotent ability to transform and redeem if I but ask.

Job 42:2
Hebrews 7:25
Matthew 28:18

Day 278

My Jesus
blesses me with beauty from His creative heart and attentively provides serene respite from the clamor of the world and its worries.

John 1:3
Revelation 4:11
John 16:33

Day 279

My Jesus
uses the furnace of adversity to burn away impurities that cloud my perception of who He is and hinder my growth as His child.

Lord,

Thank you for not wasting any pain. Thank you for using the difficult to accomplish the divine in conforming me to yourself. Continue helping me grow by removing whatever obstacles, misconceptions, or lapses in faith that stand between your heart and mine. Thank you for faithfully completing your work in me.

Amen.

Day 280

My Jesus
mercifully exonerated me although
His holiness declared me unrighteous,
His righteousness sought justice, and
His law demanded punishment.

Isaiah 44:22
James 2:10
Jeremiah 17:9

Day 281

My Jesus
is the compassionate friend, faithful companion, and invincible champion who is with me and for me now and always.

Psalm 89:8
Psalm 86:15
Jeremiah 20:11

Day 282

My Jesus
permeates the prideful intellect, pierces the resistant soul, and transforms the bitter heart with His everlasting truth, irrefutable revelation, and irresistible love.

Acts 22:3-10
Acts 9:5
1 John 3:1a

Day 283

My Jesus

is gracious to pardon my sin, patient to continue shaping me into His image, and merciful to one day welcome me into paradise.

Exodus 34:6-7
Hebrews 12:9-11
Revelation 2:7

Day 284

My Jesus
softens hearts of stone, enflames hearts of ice, and rescues hearts languishing in stagnant pools of indifference.

Lord,

Your power to change hearts is astonishing. That you can take into your loving hands a hard, cold heart and make it new is beautiful proof of who you are. That you can transform an uncaring heart into one that loves like you love is yet more proof that you can do all things. Thank you for transforming my heart so that it beats for you.

Amen.

Day 285

My Jesus
strengthens me to dig deeper, reach higher, and keep moving forward in His power when the enemy pressures me to stop, pull back, and give up.

Philippians 4:13
James 4:7
Philippians 3:13-14

Day 286

My Jesus

gives me peace with what has been, courage to face what is, and eager anticipation for what can be because He was, is, and is to come.

Isaiah 43:18-19

Hebrews 13:5b-6

Revelation 1:8

Day 287

My Jesus
has the sovereign right to do what He chooses
in my life, and I can trust that everything
He does is good, wise, and perfect.

1 Timothy 6:15b
Psalm 135:6
Deuteronomy 32:4

Day 288

My Jesus
helps me become more like Him
by teaching, refining, and igniting
within me an inextinguishable fervor
for insight, wisdom, and truth.

2 Corinthians 3:18
Isaiah 48:10
Psalm 119:43

Day 289

My Jesus
continually assures me that the truth is true no matter how I feel, no matter the challenges I face, and no matter the lies the enemy hurls at me.

Lord,

I am grateful you are unchanging and that it is upon your truth I stand firmly, no matter my mood, circumstances, or the enemy's attempted deception. Thank you for setting me securely upon the rock that is everlasting. And thank you for holding me there. Forever.

Amen.

Day 290

My Jesus
resides with me in troubles, helps me trust Him when I cannot see a way through, and promises to use my trials to bless others with the same cherished comfort I receive.

Psalm 138:7
Isaiah 50:10
2 Corinthians 1:4

Day 291

My Jesus
is in command of my every circumstance, and every outcome is anchored in His wisdom, omnipotence, and boundless love.

Romans 11:33-36
John 3:16
Revelation 19:6

Day 292

My Jesus
brings new days that dawn with fresh mercy,
renewed strength, and bright hope.

Lamentations 3:22-23
Isaiah 40:31
Hebrews 10:23

Day 293

My Jesus
never rations His grace in me, never limits His mercy toward me, and never withdraws His love from me.

John 1:16
Ephesians 2:4-5
Psalm 136

Day 294

My Jesus
is so enthralling and His love so fulfilling
that to walk away from Him is unthinkable
for those who truly know Him.

Lord,

As I grow in deeper fellowship with you, I am increasingly nourished, strengthened, and filled. I believe without a doubt that you are everything I need and that your faithfulness keeps me walking with you now and forever.

Amen.

Day 295

My Jesus
commands obedience, not as a harsh taskmaster, but as a gentle encourager and faithful provider of spiritual strength.

1 Peter 1:14-15
Matthew 11:29
2 Thessalonians 2:16-17

Day 296

My Jesus
grieves over those who choose to remain in shackles when forgiveness, freedom, and faith await them at the foot of the cross.

Mark 3:5
Galatians 5:1
Isaiah 61:1

Day 297

My Jesus
is the author of a sacred story that
fills the soul, renews the mind, and
comforts the heart infinitely beyond
what any work of man could ever do.

2 Timothy 2:16-17
Hebrews 4:12
Psalm 94:19

Day 298

My Jesus
resurrected my dead soul, called me out of sin's grave, and set my feet securely on the path of victorious eternal life.

Colossians 2:13
Psalm 16:11
1 Corinthians 15:57

Day 299

My Jesus
is the word of God that is true, the peace of God that is real, and the power of God that is forever triumphant.

Lord,

Time and again you confirm your word as unchanging truth. It always provides peace. It never fails to remind that your power is always triumphant. Thank you for the priceless and powerful confidence in your character that you convey to us in scripture.

Amen.

Day 300

My Jesus
is the Savior who delivers me, the victor who conquers for me, and the protector who wraps me safely in His omnipotent care.

Psalm 144:2
Exodus 14:14
Psalm 121:8

Day 301

My Jesus

pours serenity into the troubled places of the mind, weaves paths of healing through the jagged terrain of the wounded heart, and nourishes the soul with sustenance that satisfies its deepest hunger.

Romans 8:6
Jeremiah 17:14
Psalm 81:10b

Day 302

My Jesus
overwhelms me with the depth of His mercy, the finality of His forgiveness, and the magnitude of His transforming grace.

1 Timothy 1:15-16
Psalm 103:12
Ezekiel 36:26

Day 303

My Jesus
invites me to continually draw from the springs of His salvation the refreshing mercies of divine rescue, gracious forgiveness, and incomparable peace.

Isaiah 12:2-3
2 Corinthians 1:9-10
Psalm 32:2

Day 304

My Jesus
assures me that when I see Him
face to face, all my questions will be
answered, or they will no longer matter
in the splendor of His presence.

Lord,

Your whispered encouragement reminds me that you preside over all events and outcomes and that someday I will understand your ways. You gently remind me that in your presence every question will either be answered or carried away on wings of eternal wisdom and divine peace. Such utter tranquility I cannot fathom but anticipate joyfully. Thank you for these gifts.

Amen.

Day 305

My Jesus
removed my sin so far from me that it shall never again be linked to me, never again imprison me, and never again separate me from Him.

Isaiah 43:25
Isaiah 61:1
Isaiah 43:13

Day 306

My Jesus
is the promise of life beyond this life, joy despite these present circumstances, and in hardship, peace that no words can recount.

Romans 8:18-25
1 Peter 1:8-9
Philippians 4:7

Day 307

My Jesus
is the rock that pours forth living water to satisfy my spiritual thirst, and He is the unending source of manna from heaven that feeds my soul with all His good gifts.

Psalm 107:9
John 6:51
1 Corinthians 10:1-4

Day 308

My Jesus
blesses me with the gifts of salvation and faith, priceless treasures from His heart that power my perseverance and inspire expectant prayer.

2 Corinthians 9:15
Hebrews 10:36-39
Luke 11:9-10

Day 309

My Jesus
is King over and in me no matter
what is happening around me.

Lord,

Your kingship over me and your powerful presence in me help me trust rather than worry. Knowing that you are good and work things together for my good enables me to rest rather than wring my hands over any situation. Thank you for your presence, power, and promises that settle me.

Amen.

Day 310

My Jesus
emanates harmony, authenticity, and compassion that triumph over human strife, manipulation, and disregard for others.

Colossians 3:14
1 John 5:20
Psalm 145:8

Day 311

My Jesus
is fire that will consume His enemies,
and yet is warmth that comforts my soul
and radiant light that dispels darkness.

Psalm 92:9
John 1:5
Psalm 18:28

Day 312

My Jesus
inspires joyful laughter and jubilant rejoicing
that echo throughout heaven in a chorus
of praise untainted by earthly worries, all
sorrow forgotten and all pain erased.

Jude 24-25
John 16:22
Revelation 21:3-4

Day 313

My Jesus
is my invincible strength, merciful deliverance, and unshakeable fortress— my highest hope for today and forever.

Psalm 89:6-9
Acts 7:9-10
Titus 3:7

Day 314

My Jesus
holds my heart gently in His hands,
saving my tears in His bottle and
treasuring my joyous moments.

Lord,

Not only do you bless me with many occasions to laugh joyfully, but when I remember that you also delight in the sound, I am even more blessed. Thank you that I experience love and lightheartedness because my heart is safe in your hands. And when not all is joy, when my heart aches and tears fall, I know that you share my pain and count each tear precious.

Amen.

Day 315

My Jesus
is my insightful counselor who brings timely wisdom, clarity, and peace of mind as I pray about and think through complex issues and difficult situations.

Romans 11:33
Psalm 119:165
James 3:17

Day 316

My Jesus
shows me that His blessings follow my obedience, His wisdom is bestowed when humbly sought, and His love is not earned but freely given.

Isaiah 1:19
James 4:12
Isaiah 26:7

Day 317

My Jesus
knows what is needed to sculpt my soul into a vessel suited for fulfilling His kingdom purpose, and He orchestrates my life accordingly.

Jeremiah 18:1-6
Romans 8:28
Isaiah 10:23

Day 318

My Jesus
makes His presence known when He convicts me of sin, whispers comfort to my soul, and urges me to a righteousness far beyond my humanness.

Revelation 3:19
Psalm 119:50
2 Corinthians 4:7

Day 319

My Jesus
is a fire in my soul that sustains me now
and a dazzling star on the far horizon
of this life beckoning me to the next
when in glory He shall meet me.

Lord,

Thank you for encouraging, strengthening, and carrying me now, and thank you for faithfully keeping your promise of salvation that assures me of eternity with you. Looking forward to the culmination of that promise makes the here and now purposeful and hope-filled, and it also fixes my focus on that far horizon. Oh glorious day!

Amen.

Day 320

My Jesus
guides me when I seek His direction, shelters me in His mighty arms when I stay close to Him, and speaks peace to my heart through the outpouring of His word.

Psalm 16:8-11
Psalm 119:114
John 15:4-5

Day 321

My Jesus
is my ever-present hope, my blood-bought forgiveness, and my sure and settled salvation.

Psalm 71:5
1 Corinthians 6:20
Psalm 119:89-90a

Day 322

My Jesus
demonstrates unlimited power that can never be surpassed, He possesses fathomless knowledge that can never be refuted, and He embodies divine perfection that can never be altered.

Jeremiah 32:27
Isaiah 40:28
Matthew 5:48

Day 323

My Jesus
reveals to me that all the good in me is His spirit in me, that He alone is the reason I am redeemed, and that there is no place for pride at His table of grace.

Romans 11:6
Ephesians 2:8-9
James 4:6

Day 324

My Jesus
changes the desires of my heart for my good, gives me dreams for my life that reflect His heart, and guides my steps with wisdom to follow His path.

Lord,

Thank you for continually transforming the desires of my heart into those which honor you. You have shown me that your plans for me far surpass what I can orchestrate on my own, and the dreams you impart bring unimagined blessings, miraculous healing, and eternal joy. Thank you for intervening in my life and plans so beautifully.

Amen.

Day 325

My Jesus
redeemed me with His blood, a treasure more precious than silver or gold, purer than the whitest snow, and mightier than all the forces of evil.

1 Peter 1:18-19
Colossians 2:14-15
Revelation 7:14

Day 326

My Jesus
allowed me to find Him, drew me to repentance, and ever so gently embraces me in my brokenness as He sets about healing it.

Acts 17:24-27
Luke 5:31-32
Psalm 30:2

Day 327

My Jesus
is the lens through which I view life as I
learn that only by His truth will I perceive
accurately, discern properly, and choose wisely.

Daniel 12:3
1 Corinthians 2:14-16
James 3:17

Day 328

My Jesus
is my heart's safest shelter, the wellspring
of my mind's deepest thoughts, and
my soul's highest, purest love.

Isaiah 25:4a

Psalm 92:5

Psalm 108:4

Day 329

My Jesus
supernaturally imparts renewed zeal, profound purpose, and glorious hope to the soul suffering from aimlessness and despair.

Lord,

It is truly a miracle how you renew a life by igniting a heavenly fervor within the discouraged soul and overflow the despairing heart with joyous regeneration. Only you can accomplish such an extraordinary metamorphosis. I praise and thank you for your transformative power.

Amen.

Day 330

My Jesus
is the only light that illuminates the darkness, the only love that draws hearts to salvation, and the only power that delivers souls from death.

Psalm 139:12
1 John 4:10
Psalm 116:8

Day 331

My Jesus
hung on the cross between mercy and judgment, perfectly displaying His divine position as merciful mediator and just judge.

Luke 23:39-43
1 Timothy 2:5-6
Psalm 96:11-13

Day 332

My Jesus
empowers me to tear down the idols of my heart, trust Him unreservedly, and humbly walk with Him in gratefulness for His blessing upon my every endeavor that honors Him.

Psalm 24:3-4
Hebrews 12:28
Proverbs 16:3

Day 333

My Jesus
redeems my trials by using them to increase my knowledge of Him, strengthen my faith, and equip me to help others navigate their own challenges.

Psalm 119:71
Hebrews 12:11
2 Corinthians 1:4

Day 334

My Jesus
changes my fears into faith in His omnipotence, my doubts into confidence in His goodness, and my questions into assurance that He knows all things.

Lord,

As you whittle away at my fears and doubts, you graciously gift me with faith that counteracts fear and with belief in your unwavering goodness that displaces doubt. My uncertainties melt away in light of these divine gifts, and the assurance of your omniscience is but another gift from your generous heart.

Amen.

Day 335

My Jesus
is the defense of my soul, the desire of
my heart, and the delight of my life.

Psalm 27:1

Psalm 84:10

Psalm 119:16

Day 336

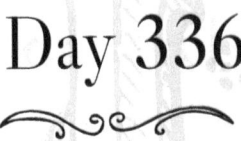

My Jesus
is a teacher who instructs me, an encourager who cheers me on, and a confidant who is always present with a compassionate heart for my every concern.

Psalm 32:8
Matthew 24:13
Psalm 17:6-7

Day 337

My Jesus
shows me that when I release control, humbly allow Him to lead, and joyfully step into His storyline, He replaces my fretting with faith and my worry becomes wonder at His consummate power.

1 Peter 5:6
Proverbs 19:21
Psalm 40:5

Day 338

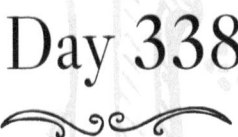

My Jesus
shows me that serving Him is not about following a list of rigid, stifling rules but about honoring Him in all I do as an outpouring of my gratefulness for who He is and what He has done.

2 Corinthians 3:5-6
Mark 7:6-8
2 Corinthians 16:14

Day 339

My Jesus
is always near, shielding me in fearful times, comforting me in difficult times, and rejoicing with me in cheerful times.

Lord,

When fear threatens, I hear your calming voice whispering from your word: "Do not fear." When trials come, I experience your comforting power and gentle reassurance that you have it all in hand. And when times of rejoicing come, I am thankful for you as the source of every good gift.

Amen.

Day 340

My Jesus
is the word of life that saved me, the wisdom
of God that guides me, and the certainty
of eternity with Him that fortifies me.

John 6:68
Proverbs 9:1
Titus 1:2

Day 341

My Jesus
is the generous Savior who evokes gratitude for all He has done in the past, causes me to joyfully watch for His works in the present, and sparks eager expectancy for what He has in store.

Psalm 44:8
Psalm 105:2
Isaiah 43:19

Day 342

My Jesus
became a human because I needed a sympathetic high priest, He was crucified because I needed a perfect sacrifice for my sin, and He came back to life because only the One who defeated death could give me eternal life.

Hebrews 4:15
Hebrews 9:22
2 Timothy 1:10

Day 343

My Jesus
is the eternal word that is veiled, puzzling,
and offensive to the lost yet discernible,
enlightening, and delightful to the redeemed.

2 Corinthians 4:3
1 Peter 2:7-8
2 Corinthians 3:15

Day 344

My Jesus
strengthens my soul to persevere when circumstances test, refreshes my spirit through communion with Him in prayer, and moves my heart to rejoice always in His wondrous, eternal hope.

Lord,

Only because of you am I able to put one foot in front of the other. Only because of how you infuse me with strength and refresh my spirit am I able to persevere. And only because you bestow hope beyond my circumstances am I able to rise above them and cling to your everlasting promises. Thank you.

Amen.

Day 345

My Jesus
is the only hope for this world because
He is the only One who brings purpose
out of suffering, transforms hate-
filled hearts into vessels of love, and
liberates souls trapped in darkness.

1 Peter 4:12-16
Ezekiel 36:26
Luke 4:18-19

Day 346

My Jesus
is lovely yet dreadfully fierce, compassionate yet a consuming fire, and patient yet arrayed to rule the nations with an iron scepter.

Psalm 27:4

Revelation 19:15

Hebrews 12:29

Day 347

My Jesus
answers prayers out of His storehouse of infinite knowledge, supreme wisdom, and generous character rather than according to my limited knowledge, human understanding, and often self-centered desires.

Proverbs 2:6
Psalm 23:5
James 4:3

Day 348

My Jesus
motivates me to seek Him with all my heart, soul, mind, and strength because He alone fulfills all my emotional, spiritual, mental, and physical needs.

Luke 12:22-32
Matthew 6:31-33
Isaiah 26:3

Day 349

My Jesus

views me through the lens of His generous favor, enduring compassion, and boundless love, focusing on His redeeming work in my life as He makes me more like Him.

Lord,

Your favor shelters me, your compassion heals me, and your boundless love sets my soul aflame. Thank you for your goodness that sees me through merciful eyes and seeks to change me into your image while accepting me as I am, a mercy that is wholly undeserved but heartily treasured.

Amen.

Day 350

My Jesus
tenderly responds to prayers lifted only in my thoughts, the wordless laments of my sin-wounded heart, and the inexpressible pleas of my needy soul.

Psalm 139:4
Matthew 6:8b
Romans 8:26-27

Day 351

My Jesus
willingly stepped into humanity, His glory veiled in skin, His majesty marked by humility, and His power in absolute command of every action against Him.

Luke 22:41-42
Philippians 2:8
John 8:20

Day 352

My Jesus
gives good gifts, ever the perfect Father who delights in answering prayers and providing for the needs of His children.

James 1:17
Isaiah 9:6
Matthew 7:11

Day 353

My Jesus
is so great a Savior that when I contemplate His profound majesty, unlimited power, and indescribable love, I am both speechless and overflowing with heartfelt praise.

Psalm 145:3
Psalm 96:6
Jeremiah 20:9

Day 354

My Jesus
delights in me as if I had never mocked Him, walks with me as if I had never betrayed Him, and loves me as if I had never broken His heart.

Lord,

The mercy you have showered upon me, the grace you have extended to me, and the forgiveness you have poured out on me render me awestruck. I remember what I once was. I recall with sorrowful regret my mocking and ignorant disregard for parts of your word. Yet you, in unfathomable love, have chosen to forgive and forget. And you love me still. Thank you.

Amen.

Day 355

My Jesus
compels me to reject the lesser offerings
of the world, the dangerous temptations
of the enemy, and the selfish inclinations
of my heart so that I may become
truly fulfilled, holy, and selfless.

Matthew 6:20
Matthew 6:13
Philippians 2:3-4

Day 356

My Jesus
is such a king that there are none wiser,
such a friend that there are none kinder,
and such a redeemer that there is no other.

Romans 16:27
Luke 6:35
Acts 4:12

Day 357

My Jesus
fashions new thoughts, inspires changed behaviors, and bestows transcendent hope to marvelously reshape lives in unimaginable ways.

Philippians 4:8-9
Ephesians 4:21-24
1 Corinthians 15:16-21

Day 358

My Jesus
is love personified, forgiveness exemplified, and my soul justified.

1 John 4:8
Luke 23:34
Romans 3:23-24

Day 359

My Jesus
makes broken things new, empty
things filled, and dead things alive.

Lord,

Only you have the power and compassion to mend the heart that is broken, fill the soul that is empty, and bring new life to what sin has destroyed. What hope and triumph, what delight and contentedness are mine in you. Thank you.

Amen.

Day 360

My Jesus
gives clean slates, fresh starts,
and rekindled hope.

2 Corinthians 5:17
Psalm 51:7
Romans 6:4

Day 361

My Jesus
causes me to yearn for heaven, not for the mansion He has prepared nor the crown He promises, but for His sweet presence reigning in eternal glory.

John 14:3
2 Timothy 2:11
1 Thessalonians 4:17

Day 362

My Jesus
is the word that is a weapon of war and an instrument of peace, a powerful sword and a healer of wounds, and a stone of offense for the lost yet the rock of truth that undergirds the saved.

Isaiah 9:6
Psalm 107:20
1 Peter 2:7-8

Day 363

My Jesus
teaches me that I am not identified by
my temptations, mistakes, or failures
but by His redemption, righteousness,
and victory in and for me.

Galatians 2:20
Romans 4:7
1 Corinthians 15:57

Day 364

My Jesus
is irrefutable truth, irresistible love,
and exhilarating freedom.

Lord,

I am deeply grateful that in this ever-changing world, your truth remains the same. I am thankful my soul yearns for your love because it knows what it needs most. And I rejoice in the liberty you bestow that gives my soul wings to soar above worldly cares.

Amen.

Day 365

My Jesus
is the one constant to which I cling as the minutes and years roll by, as people change and circumstances challenge, and when life requires more than I can give.

Isaiah 41:10
Numbers 23:19
Psalm 70:5

Day 366

My Jesus
changed the calendar with His birth,
the religious status quo with His
life, and my eternal destiny with
His death and resurrection.

Genesis 1:1 - Revelation 22:21

Gracious Lord,

No words can adequately describe the magnitude of your impact upon me and upon the world. How does the Creator impact the created? Impact is surely too small a word. From creation, to your birth, to your death and resurrection, to all of eternity, my life and the lives of every person and every thing that has ever existed are touched and held together by your exemplary love and incomparable power. The truly fortunate souls are transformed by this love and power. We are also changed by your extravagant kindness, fathomless mercy, and selfless sacrifice. May we never take any of your gifts for granted. Thank you from the depths of this soul that is forever changed from death unto life.

Thank you for being my Jesus.

Amen.

My Jesus, the Christ

Stepped down from glory
Became a child
Taught the teachers
Spoke the truth

Comforted the crowds
Fed the multitudes
Rebuked the devil
Wept for the lost

Exposed the hypocrites
Chastised the proud
Chose the unexpected
Upended religion

Healed the sick
Repaired the broken
Freed the captives
Raised the dead

Exalted the humble
Cared for the rejects
Touched the untouchables
Defended the condemned

Listened to thoughts
Spoke to hearts
Encouraged the downcast
Blessed the faithful

Prayed for His followers
Submitted to the Father
Commanded all moments
Fulfilled the law

Received our stripes
Wore the crown
Carried the cross
Accepted the nails

Bore our sin
Cried out in sorrow
Forgave the guilty
Bled and died

Canceled our debt
Rent the veil
Shook the earth
Opened the graves

Finished the plan
Lay in the tomb
Rose to life
Walked out of the grave

Commissioned disciples
Promised His presence
Ascended to glory
Now reigns on His throne.

Janice Powell

Suggestions for Going Deeper

1. To help you focus on the scripture content, write verses in a notebook or journal or write them on index cards to help you memorize them.

2. Note any unfamiliar words in the scriptures and look them up in a Bible dictionary or Greek/Hebrew lexicon.

3. Compare the verses or passages in a few different translations.

4. Explore the contexts of the scriptures to gain deeper understanding. Who is speaking? Who is addressed?

5. Search for additional verses or passages that refer to the attributes in the daily readings.

6. Look for other attributes of Jesus in the referenced scriptures that are not specifically referenced in the declaration.

7. Copy the declaration and consider how understanding the particular truth affects your view of the Savior. How did it change?

8. Consider what the scriptures say about Jesus and ponder how knowing those things changes you. What will you ask the Lord to change in your life for having known these things?

9. Copy the prayers and add your own praises and petitions.

10. Write your own *My Jesus* testimonies from what you learn through your study.

Acknowledgments

Many friends have inspired me with uplifting comments that the words I write encourage them. They, along with other readers, urged me to publish these *My Jesus* writings in book form. I am thankful for their support and inspiration.

To my artist daughter Kaylyn, thank you for sharing your gift and helping me realize my long-held dream of collaborating on a book with you.

Thank you to Mark, a Christian brother in Texas, who freely offered his editing expertise on this project because he believes in the message and the Savior who inspired it. I am grateful for his many hours of labor, kind encouragement, and grammar lessons that challenged me to write more clearly. With that said, dear reader, any errors are my own and I apologize should you find any.

Finally, thank you to my husband Ted who encourages me to pursue my passion for the written word. Although as a left-brained mechanic he does not relate to my love of words, he responds to everything I write with "Wow!" or "Amen!" He was by my side for seven births. He has faithfully provided for me to be a full-time mom and homemaker. And he has spent countless hours by my hospital beds or waiting in plastic chairs through my many medical procedures. Now, that is love.

Gratefully,
Janice

About the Author

JANICE K. POWELL grew up in the Missouri Ozarks, but Oklahoma has been home almost since she and Ted were newlyweds. When he landed his airline dream job, the couple loaded up their yellow Chevy truck and red Oldsmobile with their meager belongings and two cats and headed west.

Janice encountered Christ at VBS at age 9, and since then, the Lord has mercifully worked on growing her up in Him. With several health issues diagnosed in recent years, she is a frequent flyer at various doctor's offices and hospitals and is grateful for the Lord's strength and faithfulness to hold her together throughout her journey.

She is fascinated with words and seeks to arrange them in ways that draw readers to Christ, bring a smile, spark a profound thought, and inspire hope. When she is not writing, Janice enjoys walking on low-humidity days, admiring sunsets, playing the piano, drinking tea, and (desperately) finding ways to make chocolate healthier.

Previously published work is *Blessings for Mothers,* Barbour Publishing Inc., 2010. Janice also contributed to *Blissfully Blended,* Barbour Publishing Inc., 2010.

Connect with Janice: janicekpowell.com
Facebook and X: @wordsbeyondme

About the Artist

KAYLYN POWELL STACY is a multidisciplinary artist from Oklahoma with a background in illustration and draftsman style drawing. She is currently traveling the country painting murals as half of a partnership entitled RoadRunner Murals. For inquiries, she may be reached at kpowellrrm@gmail.com.

www.ingramcontent.com/pod-product-compliance
Lightning Source LLC
Chambersburg PA
CBHW030450100526
44580CB00002B/66